# Tool Box Kit

# PERSEVERANCE
## WINNER BY A KNOCK OUT

## Stacy D. Coward, RN, LPC

*Tree House Ministries Publishing*

Tree House Ministries Publishing Products are available at special quantity for bulk purchases for the sales and promotions premium fundraiser and educational needs. For more details write to 3615 Victory Blvd Portsmouth, Virginia 23704 or email stacy.coward@yahoo.com.

*This book is written for all the people who are trying to gain the skills of perseverance. It is practical tool with real applications that work through motivational counseling technique that will help you to continue in your journey of life. It is written to empower, influence and encourage you when you feel like giving up!*

# The Pep Talk

Listen to me son
You are going into the fight of your life
Everything you do in this fight will count
It may get tough
You may even feel a little scared but
Best believe
Everyone is rooting for you!
This is YOUR fight
The battle is not yours but the fight belongs to
you

I can't want it for you
You have to want it
You declare
You decree
You decide
You choose
You work
You study
You show yourself APPROVED

The fight may get hard
That's when you wrestle with IT
That's when you talk to IT
That's when you deal with IT
IT
IT
IT
Whatever your It is
It lives in my mind

IT is
Your past
Your pain
Your anger
Your trust issues
Your sad stories
Your stuff
When you are in the struggle and you see
yourself falling
Hit the Reset button by Acting as though you
already ARE

If you ACT like IT you will become IT

IT
IT
IT

You get to choose your IT in this fight

IT is
Your future
Your happy days
Your success
Your new stories
Your treasures

Ding, Ding, Ding
Jump Up
Act Motivated
Act Strong
Act Confident
Act like you are well able to take on your
opponent

Here we go!
The fight is on

Hate verses Love
Jail verses Job
Streets verses Home
Books verses Games
Baby Mama's verses Wives
Community Leader verse Gang Member
Attorney verses Convict
Ex-Military verses Ex-Felon


This is    HISTORY    in the making

Yes! HIS story in the making

# Round One

One, two, three, duck, weave, bob- repeat
One, two, three, duck, weave, bob- repeat
Yes, I finally made it
I am in the fight of my life

I believe I can do it

Duck, weave and bob

Get out of the way

Punch when I need to

And keep my feet moving

Ding, Ding, Ding
Jump Up
Act Motivated
Act Strong
Act Confident
Act like you are well able to take on your
opponent

Thump, Thump
I bump my gloves together
I swing my arms back and forth
Jump up and down a few times
Show him what I'm working with
Let him know I'm motivated
Let him know I'm strong
Let him know I'm confident


I got the eye the tiger
I am ready
Give him my number two combination move
I practice that one
Whoa!
This dude can fight
He is stronger than I thought

Keep jabbing
Duck, weave, bob
Duck, weave, bob

Oh no!
I am stuck on the rope
Take a few body blows

Stand
Take a few head blows
Stand
I feel weak in the legs
I must stand!

Keep jabbing
Duck, weave, bob
Duck, weave, bob

My stomach feels queezy
Embarrassing me
My breaths feel wheezy
I can barely see
My head is spinning
I'm sort of dizzy

My heart is pounding
I think I'm bleeding
My lip is throbbing
His glove just kissed me

Left, Right, jab, jab
Keep Moving
Take the full body blows


But Keep Moving
It hurts
I gotta keep moving

Stand up, shake it off
Keep fighting
I'm scared what if
Screw a "what if"
Fight!

Don't Bow
Don't Bend
I'm tired
Screw "Tired"
Fight some more!
Punches from the left, right, top and bottom
I can't take......
Screw "can't"
Fight like your life depends on it!

Keep jabbing
Duck, weave, bob
Duck, weave, bob
Ha-Ha
He missed me!
That was close

# The Pep Talk

He is weak on his left side

Remember to guard your weak side
Don't act afraid in there
Watch his eyes they will tell you his next move
Here have some water


Ding, Ding, Ding
Jump Up
Act Motivated
Act Strong
Act Confident
Act like you are well able to take on your
opponent

# Round Two

This will be easy I only have to

Punch back
Hit hard
Be Precise
Duck
Stay low
Stay tight
Jab, jab

I hear it in a distant
"Keep your chin tucked!"
I'm losing my breath
I 'm tired

This is more than I thought

I didn't think it would be this hard
I may have underestimated him
When is the bell going ring?
I'm tired
Jab, Jab, duck weave, bob

Did he just punch me in my eye?
Now what?

Ding, Ding, Ding,
Rest
Drink water

# The Pep Talk

You can do it
You are strong
You are built for this
You almost had him that time
Get in there and do it again
This time you can take him

Ding, Ding, Ding
Jump Up
Act Motivated
Act Strong
Act Confident
Act like you are well able to take on your
opponent

# Round Three

Move your feet
Guard Yourself
Keep your elbows tight

Protect your weak spots
Don't let him punch me in that spot it hurts
I'm tired.
I am hurting
I want to give up
Ouch! That hurt
Now, I am mad
Stay focus I can't win mad
Remember my technique
Remember my training

# *Focus*

Wait for the perfect time
Wait for it
Wait for it
Move your feet while you are waiting

Protect yourself
Get through the round
Jab, jab, bob and weave

Thirty more seconds
I can make it
I just have to keep my feet moving

*Ding, Ding, Ding,*
*Rest*
*Drink water*

# The Pep Talk

You are ready for this
You can do it
This is what you have been training for all these
years
You are well able to conquer him
You are a warrior
You have God on your side

Ding, Ding, Ding
Jump Up
Act Motivated
Act Strong
Act Confident
Act like you are well able to take on your
opponent

# Round Four

My strength flees from me
All I have is a
Punch
Hold
Punch
Hold
Punch
Hold
Hold
Hold
Punch
I gave it my all!

<br><br>

# Ding, Ding, Ding,
## Rest
## Drink water

# The Pep Talk

Take some deep breaths
Concentrate on your breathing
Pace yourself
Don't exert all your energy
You almost got him

Ding, Ding, Ding
Jump Up
Act Motivated
Act Strong
Act Confident
Act like you are well able to take on your
opponent

# The Final Round

The fight is almost over
Did I give my all?
Did I stand?
Did I get up?
Did I take the hard licks?
Did I fight fair?
Did I keep clean hands?
Did I make my mama proud?
Did I do it Right?
Did I lead with the right kind of hands?
Did step forward after a hard hit?
Who will the people say I am?
No, No, No, better question
Who will my children say I am?

Ding, Ding, Ding,
Rest
Drink water

## The Winners Talk

I'm bleeding

*No worries*

I can't see

*No worries*

I think he broke my ribs

*No worries*

I'm sore everywhere

*No worries*

It hurts to breathe

*No worries*

I'm covered in Oil

*No worries*

I can get through this fight

Ding, Ding, Ding
Jump Up
Act Motivated
Act Strong
Act Confident
Act like you are well able to take on your
opponent

# The Deciding Round

Punch, jab, duck, weave, bob
Move your feet
Watch your breathing
Concentrate
Can't afford to be mad
The Oil works
Use the techniques
Hold on him
Catch your breath
Use the training
All my life trained for this day

Take the body blow
Ouch, Ah, the pain
Take the head blow
I see stars
My ears are ringing
Stand
I feel wobbly but I'm still up
Sort of
Stay off the ropes
Watch out for traps
Keep moving
No matter what
Don't stand still

I'm waiting on the
Ding, Ding, Ding,
Rest
Drink water moment

I could use a break

# But until then

Punch with all my might
Give everything I got
Be Precise
Strike
Lightening Fast
He will never know what hit him

# But until then

Where is the
Ding, Ding, Ding,
Rest
Drink water moment?

# But until then

Keep breathing

Deep breath in
Deep breath out
Deep breath in
Deep breath out
Deep breath in
Deep breath out
Out,
Out,
Out,

The room is dark
10, 9, 8, 7, 6, 5


Are they counting down on me?

That is for me!
Did he just knock me
Out,
Out,
Out?

I think so
It's hard to tell
I can't tell
It's all a big blur
It went so fast
Yeah, the room is spinning
How did I get knocked down?


Lord, remind me of those words?

Jump Up
Act Motivated
Act Strong
Act Confident
Act like you are well able to take on your
opponent

You can't stay down there!

The ref is counting
He's neutral
The clock is ticking
It's the same clock for everybody

The people are shouting
Past, present and future
From great, great, grandma nem' to your great,
great, great grand children

They peer over the heavenly balcony
Waiting to see.... will he stand?
Ole' man says,
"Been equipped with everything he needs
He only has to use it."

Even the Heavenly Host all chant in unison
"Let the weak SAY I am strong"
"Let the weak SAY I am strong"
"Let the weak SAY I am strong"

NOBODY can stand up for you

Get Up

Best believe
Everyone is rooting for you!

BUT Don't you forget

This is YOUR fight

The battle IS NOT yours

BUT the fight belongs to you

Now Get Up

I'm on my knees

Lord I need strength

I tried standing alone

# Now

I'm standing on your Word


My way verses your way?

Remind myself to stay humble

My plans verses your plans

The Old Me verses The New Me

# Wrestle Jacob

# Israel is waiting

The "I" part of me

Oh no! You got to stay down

"I" surrender

Look!

Look!

# Look!

Legs Are Stronger
I AM up
Getting my balance
I AM up


The "I AM" in me is strong
The "I AM" in me is confident
The "I AM" in me is motivated
The "I AM" in me is well able to take on my
opponent!
" I AM" is Up

Look!

Look!

Look!

# My Opponent

Flesh

Carnality

Pride

Me, Mine and I

He's down? 10, 9, 8
I got a new beginning

He's down? 7, 6, 5
The grace was sufficient

He's down! 4, 3
Now I am made whole

Two
Double for my trouble

One

One day I can tell my children how to WIN

## Jump Up
In the power of the Lord

## Be Confident
You belong to the KING

## Be Motivated
He died for you

## You are well able to take on your opponent
When the Flesh is weak the Spirit is strong

ARMS UP!

ARMS UP?

# ARMS UP.

# Winner by a knock out!

*Dedicated to all my sons both natural and spirituals .I love you all very much and I am always praying for you!  Remember these words* **"I AM" well able to take on the opponent!**

Now get in there and fight your fight!

*Love,*
**Mama Bishop**